POSITIV

HOW TO THINK POSITIVE: THE POWER OF AFFIRMATIONS

JUSTIN ALBERT

Why I Wrote This Book

Positive thinking: it's an oft-used term in the second grade, maybe, but what does it have to do with your everyday life?

Well: according to recent research, positive thinking actually pertains to everything you do, be it at the office, in relationships, or on your own, pursuing your goals. These positive thoughts are so much more useful than the negative thoughts that toil through you—that disallow you from actualling working towards success. (Instead, when we experience negative emotions, so many of us close down, shut our eyes, and wait for that opportunity to pass us by. After all: so often, that opportunity is quite scary. Wouldn't it always be easier to continue doing the "same old, same old"?)

Personally: I wrote this book because I actually transformed my life by learning how to live with positive thoughts. This book is intended to help you lift your spirits and brighten the world around you. This book offers step-by-step processes to help you change those gut-wrenching negative emotions and beliefs into positive ones. It will help you change your negative self-esteem to positive self-esteem and low self-confidence to high self-confidence. Essentially: it forces you to flip what you know about yourself on its head.

At the end of the day, my intent is to help you become the most powerful version of yourself, to help you get out of your own way. You deserve it.

WHY YOU SHOULD READ THIS BOOK

This book will help you implement the power of positive affirmations through simple yet efficient techniques. It will guide you to condition your subconscious mind to generate positivity in different aspects of life, in areas that include confidence, self-esteem, career success, relationships, happiness, self-love, wealth, and health, and so many others.

These step-by-step techniques will provide the tools you require to achieve your goals and aspirations. This seems like a mighty thing to say, but I assure you: I know my stuff. How? In fact, I've been utilizing these techniques for the past three years in order to reach my goals, both at work and in relationships. These techniques have been my building blocks to create a better and more defined self.

As you'll see in this book, I often utilize Positive Thinking Affirmations in order to change my emotions—almost instantaneously. This has been incredibly important, nearly every day in the past three years. When I begin to feel lousy and uninspired, I remember my favorite affirmations. I use those affirmations as a sort of fuel to propel me into a better day.

Learn the strength of a positive affirmation. Learn how positive affirmations can enact remarkable change in your own life. Find a path to greatness, without spurning your brain with negativity.

After all: with negativity, you take yourself out of the equation. You allow others to win. You don't give yourself the chance to formulate the life you want.

TABLE OF CONTENTS

Chapter 1. What are Positive Affirmations?

Positive affirmations are powerful tools that help you actualize your desires in life. They are encouraging words that you tell yourself when you want to achieve a goal or simply uplift your morale. Each word that boosts your thoughts and actions is a part of the greater positive affirmation.

Modifying your mentality on failure through positive affirmation or utilizing words of encouragement instills significant positive changes in your subconscious mind in order to conquer fear of failing again. When you try to push the subconscious mind to believe that you can do what you desire, you wash away your negative mindset and create a new positive outlook.

Affirmations are usually short, positive statements that aim to resist negative thoughts, feelings, or actions. Thus, positive affirmations are aimed to replace your negative perception that hinders you from believing in yourself.

Do Positive Affirmations Work?

Indeed, positive affirmations work. In fact, you may find it difficult to find a self-help program that does not involve positive affirmations. This is because of the fact that affirmations do work in making favorable changes in one's life. All it takes is determination to change, acceptance of that change, and an ability to get rid of the past, especially past experiences that are negative.

WHY POSITIVE AFFIRMATIONS WORK?

Because positive affirmations aim to reprogram your patterns of thinking, they transform the way you feel about specific aspects of your life that you want to change. Replacing flawed beliefs with positive ones enables you to achieve positive changes naturally. As such, this positivity will begin reflecting in most aspects of your life as you experience significant, positive changes.

HOW LONG DOES IT TAKE FOR POSITIVE AFFIRMATIONS TO WORK?

The results or changes brought about by positive affirmations transpire depending on the issue you want to address and your determination to change that specific issue in your life.

Positive affirmations work more quickly when you are undoubtedly ready to make changes—when your mind is honed toward your goal. As soon as you are primed to accept change and believe it is right for you, then such change will materialize. Therefore, time is not the question. The question involves how you, personally, accept change.

HOW LONG MUST YOU DO POSITIVE AFFIRMATIONS TO CREATE CHANGE?

Positive affirmations must be done until your desired changes manifest in your life. Affirmations can be done any time, especially if you are feeling discouraged or anxious. However, affirmations can also be done, even if you feel you are already fulfilled.

When you feel discouraged, you must do affirmations that uplift you. When you feel happy, you must do affirmations that translate to continued happiness or fulfillment. Positive affirmations can be done any time and as often as you seek them to enact change.

CHAPTER 2. HOW CAN POSITIVE AFFIRMATIONS HELP TRANSFORM YOUR LIFE?

Positive affirmation is no longer a new concept; in fact, it's documented that the great Philosopher, Pythagoras taught positive affirmation to his student in the 'Pre-Socratic' times. Some say he is one of the first ancient thinkers to use the word 'philosopher'. Thus, this provides a deeper and more powerful meaning to positive affirmation—that he saw greater meaning in the positive words people can tell themselves.

In recent studies, experts have seen a relationship between positive affirmation and a human's well-being. These studies have proven the association of positive affirmation with better psychological health. Thusly, people who initiate positive affirmation generally have lower levels of anxiety, depression, and general distress, specifically in complex circumstances, such as financial instability and recovery from illnesses.

To better understand how positive affirmations are able to help you transform your life, you need to have a clear understanding of the power of your thoughts. When you continuously think about something you want, it will manifest in time. (The term "manifest" meaning, in this case, to show or demonstrate.)

Thusly, thinking encouraging and positive thoughts is absolutely essential during everyday life. Otherwise, this positivity won't manifest itself in your life.

In the same manner, when you think of only what is lacking in your life, all that will manifest is what you lack. (Negativity will naturally manifest to more negativity, more "nothingness.")

If you want to achieve your goals or desires, you need to focus on them. Positive affirmations can provide you the focus you need and lead you to the right direction. They can further give you inspiration and keep you going, even through difficult times.

Let's say your thoughts are focused on your desires. Afterwards, you combine these desiring thoughts with determination, hard work, and passion. Fairly soon, you will notice that such thoughts are manifested into reality. This is no magic. It is just how life works.

Remember that while positive affirmations help you achieve your goals or desires through encouragement and favorable thoughts, you should also take action towards achieving those goals. Positive affirmations do not magically make your dreams come true. They enable you to see things clearly. They give you the push you need to stay on the road towards your goals. Negative thoughts, on the other hand, disallow you from even walking on that road at all.

Positive affirmations attract positive opportunities; however, without appropriate actions, those opportunities towards your goals could pass you by.

A Simple Guide to Let the Power of Positive Affirmation Transform Your Life

First, on a piece of paper, write down the things you desire or want to change in your life. It is recommended to keep it personal, instead of sharing it with others. After all, more often than not, family, friends, and society tend to discourage us by saying that things cannot be done. Although they mean well, you cannot allow their discouraging words to enter your thoughts. Once you have written your desire, memorize the positive affirmation, and treat it like it already manifested or you have already achieved it.

For example, if you want to get a job that pays well—that will ultimately help you on your route to feeling validated in all the school you went through, for example, you would say the following:

"I am happy and confident in my new position that utilizes my earned skills and helps me live the life I want."

You would say it as though it has already happened, living in that "reality" for a moment.

Next, when you have time in the morning, repeat the affirmation at least 20 times, stating it with passion. Try to imagine yourself with your desire. Try to imagine how your life would be when this desire manifests into reality. At night, repeat the process prior to going to bed.

As Pythagoras insisted, philosophy must be a way of life. These positive affirmations that you have written down should be a way of life—a sort of oxygen that you wake up with, that you go to sleep with. Many of Pythagoras followers, implemented the routines very strictly to ultimately make them habits.

When you feel doubtful about your desire, clear your mind and repeat the affirmation. Discard all negative thoughts that hinder your focus from acquiring your desire.

Finally, keep your mind open to opportunities. The means of achieving your desire may not come as you have imagined them to be. Thus, you need to be alert to opportunities and take action upon them.

EXAMPLES OF POSITIVE AFFIRMATIONS FOR COMMON ISSUES

AFFIRMATIONS FOR ACTION (MOTIVATION)

The following "affirmations for action" allow you to "live in the manifestation" of walking down a successful path, making valid changes that ultimately work toward your intention. The idea is that if you "live in" the idea of the changes you're making, you'll ultimately make the changes during your everyday life.

Say the following things—perhaps making them more specific as you go, to highlight the realism. Say them in the morning and in the evening, before you go to bed.

All of my actions reveal my intentions.

My actions are geared toward my aspirations.

My actions support my desires or goals.

I bring positive outcome into my life through taking positive actions.

I take goal-directed actions each day.

AFFIRMATIONS FOR LOVE

The following affirmations hold the idea that if you give love to the universe, you will receive love back. Love is the only intangible element of the universe that humans need, the others being food, water, and oxygen.

Know that if you are searching for love, the best way to do it is to give out the same sort of love that you would like back. If you say the following affirmations—perhaps making them more specific, if you please—you'll allow your mind to live in that moment of "giving" the love you need back.

After all: it's just like the Beatles said: "And in the end, the love you take is equal to the love you make."

I give out love and love will return to me multiplied.

I deserve love and I accept it now.

I rejoice the love I receive each day.

AFFIRMATIONS FOR PEACE AND HARMONY

So often, life delivers such uproarious stress. We can never truly know what's going to "happen next" in our lives, and this continuous upheaval can create such unhappiness. Many people begin to think that if their life could end tomorrow, why should they even try toward success, toward love, toward happiness?

However, in order to be happy in every element of your life, you must accept the processes of the universe and of life. You must live with internal peace, and you must know to forgive yourself of past faults. Only with this internal peace and harmony can you pursue true change, experience love, and hold internal happiness.

I trust the process of life.

All my relationships are harmonious.

I am at peace with myself and others.

AFFIRMATIONS FOR JOY AND HAPPINESS

Why do anything if you cannot experience the true joy and happiness—joy for your decisions, joy for change, and joy for others? Life should hold its arms open for you, in acceptance of you—and only you can make that happen.

Read the following affirmations to initiate your mind into that future—that future when you allow the world to be bright and open for you. Only if you read these affirmations and allow yourself to truly believe in them can you truly hold this internal joy.

I choose joy, love, and freedom and allow favorable things to transpire in my life.

Life is full of delightful surprises.

My life is filled with fun, joy, friendship, and love.

I choose to relax, forgive, stop all criticism, and be open.

DO ALL PEOPLE USE POSITIVE AFFIRMATIONS?

Yes, everyone utilizes positive affirmations. Based on many different studies, 90% of all human thoughts are negative.

In many ways, these negative thoughts can be more powerful when compared to positive affirmations. This is because people often find that negative thoughts are easier to conform with or accept. Negative thoughts confirm your negative beliefs in yourself and in your life. This creates a sort of cyclical problem. People attempt to break free from their negative thoughts. However, they don't really believe they deserve life outside of their negative thoughts. Thusly, their negative thoughts force them back into negative beliefs. These are generally untrue. It's just, when people are faced with a wall of negativity, it can be so difficult to clamber over it and find light on the other side.

On the other hand, positive affirmations are meant to combat negative thoughts and beliefs—to be the very ladder to help you over the "wall" of negative emotions. However, beyond just repeating words and mantras, positive affirmations involve a process of awareness in thoughts AND words in your daily life—a sort of marriage. The process involves ultimately choosing to think positive thoughts and manifest them into reality. Accordingly, the more you become aware of your affirmations and instill them in your thoughts and words, the quicker they will manifest in your life.

CAN YOU USE POSITIVE AFFIRMATIONS FOR OTHER PEOPLE?

Although it is possible to invoke positive affirmations on other people, it is not a very good idea. This is because nobody knows his inner truth better than himself. In the event that you want to help others, it is best to affirm that you will be able find the right means to help or support them.

Notice above, I used the words: "Invoke positive affirmations on other people." I want to be clear about what I'm referring to here. In medieval times, many people would use affirmations to invoke these meanings on other people. They would use a phrase to frighten the other person and make them believe they had cast a sort of spell. Many hundreds of years ago—back when witch trials were much more than a Monty Python joke—these spells were utilized as incantations. These were series of words utilized to incant a belief upon you.

This still exists in modern society, as well. A concise example is found with a person using the following, mind-altering words: "You are not good enough." If you believe what that person has said, then we can say that the person has cast a spell on you—or invoked a negative affirmation in you. You allowed another persons words to affect you in a negative way.

Thusly, the only thing you can possibly do to life someone up into a positive world of thought is to make yourself available to them, allow them to understand that you're "there," that you don't believe in their negative emotions—and neither should they. However, you can't be their mantra. You can't create "incantations" with them. It's too invasive, and it probably won't work.

In the next chapter, learn the steps to create a positive affirmation: the first milestone on the road to success.

Chapter 3. Step-by-Step Creation of Positive Affirmations

Positive affirmations can be incredibly easy to create, as long as you know precisely where to begin on the journey. Remember that creating positive affirmations should be a sort of reflective period, during which you can wipe away the stressors of everyday life. I recommend doing the following steps during the evening, after a round of calmly sitting, allowing your mind to go blank. This way, you're the freshest, "blankest" version of yourself. You're ready to analyze your internal thoughts.

A Simple Process To Create Positive Affirmations

Sure, we've talked on and on about positive affirmations necessarily creating positive change in your life. However, positive affirmations can further improve your levels of energy in tremendous ways—giving you the strength to reach toward those goals. They can further improve your general satisfaction in your life.

With only a minimum span of 3 weeks, you should be able to start a habit to create and implement positive affirmations. This means that just 21 days from now, you should have the energy to change. You should view the world with a brighter mentality.

Step One: Make a List of Areas You'd Like to Improve

Initially, you must think about the specific areas or aspects in your life that you would like to change or improve. These can involve anything. Do you wish you had a better relationship with your wife? Do you wish you had a better position at work? Do you wish you were thinner and healthier, rather than overweight?

Think about how you want these areas to change. After you've narrowed down a solid list of things you want to change about yourself, you must make a list. Writing them down is an essential step on the road to realizing where you hold negativity in your brain. When you see them out on paper, they're no longer such a "part" of you. Rather, they're something you can alter, can change.

STEP 2: MAKE USE OF AN ENCOURAGING VOCABULARY

On the list, take note of each area. Begin to read into your mind and think about a future during which you will have already achieved some of these things. Begin to write a few words of encouragement or positive statements about each section. These words should focus what the things you want, rather than things family members want for you, friends want for you. These words should bleed out your internal desires.

For instance, if you want to achieve success in your career, your positive affirmation could be, "I have a great job that brings me to higher levels of life."

If you want to achieve success in your health, your positive affirmation could be: "I am healthy and happy in my own skin as a result of good, healthy choices."

Remember: no one else should create your positive affirmations for you. You are the only one who understands your inner desires and how you want them to manifest themselves in your life.

STEP 3: MAKE A LIST OF CURRENT BEAUTIFUL AREAS OF YOUR LIFE

After you've decided on the areas in which you'd like to affect great change, it's essential that you take a moment to pause and think about the areas in your life that you already appreciate, that fuel you with positivity (at some level) already.

Find a clean sheet of paper to regroup. Stay in a quiet room or area in which you can clearly hear your thoughts. Close your eyes and allow your thoughts to fuel through you. Be aware of them as they pass, noting what they are, what they look like. But then: make sure that you do not judge them. Judging these thoughts and emotions vilifies them, and this is not appropriate. After all: these thoughts are a part of you. You have them for a reason.

After you've allowed your thoughts to form freely in your mind, begin to take note of every good thing in your life. Picture everything you love, every person you cherish, everything you feel that you're good at. Try to picture each element.

Know that this previous step is an incredibly important part of the process. After all: on the road to real, valid positive affirmations, it's essential that you feel good about the abundance you have in life.

STEP 4: FORM THESE BEAUTIFUL THOUGHTS INTO POSITIVE PHRASES

Write down all the elements of your life that you find beautiful. You can be as creative or as basic as you please. For example, write that you enjoy having dinner at your favorite restaurant. Write that you feel happiest during the month of May, when flowers begin to bloom. Write that you love when your son wants to play soccer with you in the backyard. Anything simple—or complex—that brings you joy: write it down.

Form each of these good, beautiful things into phrases. These phrases should be easy to repeat and easy to remember. Collect these phrases—beautiful things from your life—in a notebook that you can easily carry with you during your everyday life. This way, you can read through these affirmations of the beautiful things you already have in your life every day, when you need a morale boost. Do this alongside the aforementioned positive affirmations—the affirmations of change that you listed earlier. This way, you can feel that you're surrounded by positivity on all sides: from the present day to a future day.

Know that if you're more tech-minded, it's incredibly simple to download a "Notes App" to your phone and make your affirmation lists there. This way, you can have your list on your person all the time. Rather than looking at cat videos (which are, assuredly, very uplifting), you can read through your positive affirmations and hold a better comprehension for your goals and dreams and blessings.

SAMPLE POSITIVE AFFIRMATIONS FOR SEVEN DAYS

If you're having trouble making a list of positive affirmations for your journal, turn to the following for assistance. Remember that each day offers its new set of challenges, its new problems, its new elements seeking to downturn your moral. Rather than "go with the flow" and allow yourself to feel negativity, know that you have this list to see you through.

1. I am absolutely responsible for my life and its outcome.

2. I am worthy of happiness, wealth, and health, just because I am.

3. With every inhale, I intake positive energy. With every exhale, I release negativity.

4. I live in an abundance of joy and bliss.

5. I learn lessons as I need to, taking from them what I need to survive and live well.

6. My life is perfect, and I am grateful for every aspect of it.

7. The universe/God is always contriving for my good.

AMPLIFYING POSITIVE AFFIRMATIONS

One of the most efficient ways to amplify positive affirmations lies in stating them while facing a mirror. When you look at yourself in the eye and say your affirmation, you stress the significance of the message to yourself. This is simply common sense. After all: when people look you in the eye, they are asking you to believe in the brevity of their important messages.

OTHER TECHNIQUES TO AMPLIFY POSITIVE AFFIRMATIONS

SUBLIMINAL AFFIRMATIONS

This technique exists outside the boundaries of the conscious mind. Thusly, you might not even be directly aware of this subliminal affirmation technique.

Subliminal affirmations can be powerful because they overwhelm the ability of the mind to resist the message. You've probably heard of "subliminal" before, utilized with subliminal messages in various commercial advertisements. They're telling your unconscious mind to want something, even when your conscious mind isn't aware of it.

How does this work in the sphere of positive affirmations?

This works when you hear different voices that state positive affirmations, all from different directions—even when you do other things. Even as your conscious mind hears the voices, they'll set them to the side—allowing the "meaning" of the message to slip between the cracks, to your subconscious mind.

Do this with various products, offered with audio format and software. The audio versions tend to use soothing music alongside a person who whispers the positive words. The software flashes images of affirmations, even while you use the computer for other things. These flashes are not distracting, so you may continue to do your work at the computer as you please, allowing this positivity to wash over you. Interesting that this positivity can fuel you, even when you don't know about it. Finally: you can contact your subconscious mind utilize healthy techniques, rather than for the benefit of some sort of commercial operation.

CHANT AFFIRMATIONS

As you know already, words hold incredible power. However, the power of words is maximized when utilized for "singing" or "chanting."

Think about it. The words: "Amazing Grace, How Sweet the Sound, That Saved a Wretch Like Me." These words have incredible meaning, sure. But when they're added to the world-renowned melody, they make people cry, weep, think about their lives differently, etc. What power!

Thusly, your mind accepts affirmations with incredible ease when you're singing or chanting the words. Try singing or humming along with the thoughts of your mantras. Make up little jingles for yourself to make yourself feel grounded in your positivity, in your beliefs.

Too often, we fuel ourselves with the songs of other people, of singer-songwriters, of rock bands. Instead of brimming with other people's words, it could be essential to fill ourselves with the song of our own positivity.

In the next section, learn about how to create positive affirmations for greater confidence and self-esteem. With enhanced confidence, you have the strength to propel yourself into the life you know you deserve.

Chapter 4. Positive Affirmations for Confidence and Self-Esteem

Regardless of whether or not we're aware of it, we all have an unceasing dialogue inside our heads—one that informs our actions, what we think about things, people, events, and ourselves.

Most successful individuals claim that their subconscious, or "inner self" is on their side incessantly, giving them confidence and self-esteem affirmations. They state that these affirmations occur both when they're awake and asleep.

Thusly, we must take notes from these successful information, fueling ourselves with positivity and affirmation of our self-worth.

How Do Positive Affirmations for Confidence and self-esteem work?

In reality, the words that you tell yourself are not so different from the words that others tell you.

Think of it this way. When others tell you how unpleasant, useless, and unattractive you are, these people won't be your friends for long. Why would you want to hear those words constantly bantered to you, making you feel terrible about yourself?

However, you probably tell yourself the same things all the time through self-talk. This doesn't help your self-esteem in any way. In fact, it belittles you more than you can possibly know.

I strongly believe that no one judges you more than you judge yourself. Think about it: how often have you looked into the mirror and compared yourself to someone else? How often have you compared your "lesser-than" accomplishments to another's accomplishments? How often have you felt that you need to work out hard, dig in deeper, keep pushing—all as a result of the negative thoughts you hold in your mind?

Know this: if you don't like someone, you can walk away. If you don't like yourself, too bad. You have to carry yourself around with you, wherever you are.

Thusly, you must ask yourself the following question: are you nice to yourself? Are you guilty? Are you always prosecuting yourself?

INCREDIBLY, TENSE MATTERS

The next time you are in a stressful situation, it's essential that you think about the ways in which you "self-talk." During positive affirmations, the "first person" tense, or the "I" tense is appropriate. (After all: you're living in the moment of that positivity; you're attempting to feel all the joy of this "future" moment.)

However, research shows that the ways in which you refer to yourself during stressful situations (and when thinking about future stressful situations) actually matters on the route to reaching toward success.

According to this study, socially anxious people found that utilizing non-first person pronouns—using their own name, rather than saying the word "I," actually enhanced their ability to get through the stressful scenario. They were able to "distance" themselves from the issue and make executed, fully-formed steps to success.

Furthermore, the socially anxious people who utilized third person tense (using their own names, rather than "I"), were found to have less distress; they were found to have greater ability when meeting new people and public speaking. Furthermore, they were further shown to analyze future stressors with greater ability—looking at them as more "challenging" factors, rather than very scary events.

Thusly, the language we use with ourselves is very, very important on the route to success. When we're in the moment of stress—we're meant to use our names. For example:

"Jacob. You can do this."

When we're attempting to affect long-term change, in the formation of positive affirmation, we're meant to utilize first-person tense. For example:

"I can do this."

IDENTIFYING SELF-ESTEEM PROBLEMS

In order to push yourself out of this negative self-talk, it's essential that you identify the very real, self-esteem problems that you currently have. (They probably relate to the section earlier, during which you were meant to label the areas in your life you wish to change.)

What bothers you about yourself? Are you overweight? Do you need a better job to feel validated in your career? Does your education pale in comparison to others? What about yourself makes you stand a little shorter, makes you hang your head?

After you've identified this problem, decide—in earnest—to change these elements of your life. Do so through the positive affirmation step-by-step process, listed in a previous chapter.

Know that after you proceed with positive affirmations and work to enact change, your life and your self-esteem is again in your hands. You must change your perceptions about yourself in order to set yourself up for success, rather than failure.

LEARN POSITIVE AFFIRMATIONS FOR CONFIDENCE AND SELF-ESTEEM

As aforementioned, every person has a specific, inherent way of talking to him or herself. For example, you may repeat a specific statement all the time to yourself. Alternately, you may continually make sure that your negative statements are "in check" or appropriate "correct" by saying them to yourself over and over.

However, when you hear this negative self-talk in your mind, you must approach it immediately and halt it in its tracks.

Rather than "checking" those negative thoughts and affirming them in your mind, tell yourself the following:

"I am good enough. I am attractive. I am intelligent. I can do it."

HOW CAN YOU IMPROVE YOUR OVERALL SELF-ESTEEM: STOP COMPARING YOURSELF TO OTHERS?

When you continuously compare yourself to other people, your self-esteem takes a direct hit. This continuous comparison will not make you feel better.

However, it's true that we all do it. We're all hit with the "idealized" images of beauty and happiness and skill—with images of people who appear to have everything they've ever dreamed of.

Know, however that this behavior is, above all—relative.

Take for example an occasional basketball player. If this player compared himself to Michael Jordan, then he would definitely feel bad about himself. After all: Michael Jordan was a seasoned basketball player who put more rounds in the gym than nearly everyone else, positioning himself at the top-tier ranks of athleticism. Did this person—who is continuously comparing himself to Michael Jordan—put that many exercise and practice hours in? I'm guessing not.

Now: let's say that this occasional player compares himself to someone who does not know how to dribble or even hold a basketball—someone who, for example, takes greater pleasure out of reading about basketball than playing it. With this comparison, he might feel good about himself—where basketball is concerned, that is.

Know in this story that I am not saying that you shouldn't inspire to be as great as Michael Jordan. After all: he was the best at what he did for a very, very long time. However, if when comparing yourself to him, you feel bad about yourself, then you need to stop comparing. Instead, you must have the determination to improve each and every day—just like Michael did. (If we're all comparing ourselves to his determination, rather than to his basketball skills, perhaps we can rally our strength toward whatever our ultimate goal is!)

Know that comparing yourself to others is absolutely a learned behavior. Thusly: you weren't born with it; it was something you developed over a period of time. In order to stop this behavior, it's essential that you identify when you began comparing yourself to others. You must replace this behavior with healthy attitudes about yourself and your life. This way, you can ramp up your self-esteem.

Remember that through the following steps, you can build your self-esteem. Marry these steps with the later positive affirmations, and you'll be well on your way to greater confidence which will, in turn, help you conquer your obstacles.

The First Method: Understanding the Reason for Your Continuous Comparison

1. Ask yourself: what is your current opinion of yourself?

How do others influence your opinion of yourself? Do you find that when others do well, your opinion of yourself decreases? Do you find that when others do poorly, you feel better about yourself?

If other people determine your self-worth, then you must proceed through the following steps.

2. Know how you react when you compare yourself to others.

This involves the concept of "comparative behaviors." When this occurs, you compare either their negative or their positive elements to characteristics you have, personally.

When you compare yourself in a negative light, this can alter and damage your personal self-esteem.

Thusly, when you compare yourself to someone with qualities that you admire and wish you had, you might begin to assimilate into these qualities, as well. When someone appears to be extra fun-loving, you might, in turn, try to relax yourself a bit and "take a breather" from the stressors of the world—all because of this other person.

When this other person has something you want, but you become depressed instead of creating action to reach toward this success, you're behaving inappropriately in your comparative behavior.

3. Make a list of your comparative feelings or thoughts.

Write down everything you feel immediately after you begin to "compare" yourself to another. Note your emotions, your jealousy, your sadness, or your willingness to improve your life. And then, after you write this, make sure that you do not write another line about it. After all: dwelling on it allows the feelings to manifest.

4. Write about a time in your life when you DIDN'T compare yourself to others.

During this process, you think back throughout your life to a time during which your thoughts didn't continually drift towards others, toward others' statuses in life. Rather, you lived your life without comparison.

As you write about this time, you'll begin to remember the time in your life when these comparative thoughts began. For example, I remember the first time—fourth grade, when I first felt terrible that I didn't have the same Nike shoes as everyone else in class. What a strange, bizarre memory—one that informs so many others that came after it.

The Second Method: Learning to Replace Your Comparative Thoughts

During this process, you must learn to replace those comparative thoughts with better, more focused thoughts—thoughts that allow you to push through, to find positive affirmations, and to reach toward your goals.

1. Remember your worst failures, and laugh at them.

Everyone has failed at something. Even the most beautiful person has had an embarrassing moment; even the most successful person has lost at something.

Thusly, it's essential to remember that you, yourself, are human—even as you compare yourself to others. You must remember your most embarrassing moment and share it with your friends, learning to laugh about it. This way, your failures won't impede your growth. You can push beyond them, disallowing them from blocking you.

2. Remember to compliment others who you admire.

Each time you compare yourself to some one—to their looks, to their physical beauty—compliment them. This way, you're acknowledging what you envy in a positive way. If you do this enough, you will disallow yourself from seeing the good in others only if you compare the good with the bad in yourself. Rather, see their good and admire it—allowing them to understand your admiration. You are separate people with separate duties in this world.

3. Get off social media.

Everyone on social media presents the "idealized" version of him or herself. Nothing of their negative side is represented. And thus: you can begin to have an inappropriate comprehension of what their lives are actually like.

When you compare yourself to this "fictionalized" version of this other person, you aren't giving yourself a chance to reach toward your own goals. Rather, you're halting your progress.

Attempt, at least, to limit the amount of time on your social media accounts. Perhaps just ten minutes per day will be sufficient. However, every second that you live on social media contributes to your negative comparative thinking. Be careful.

4. Learn to think realistic thoughts.

Do not jump to conclusions about anyone or anything, and remember that anything somebody has involved a serious process. For example, if you envy someone with a really incredible job, remember the amount of work and hardship that person had to go through on the route to getting that position. If you're jealous of someone who has a really good relationship, remind yourself of how lonely this person was prior to getting into a relationship—and feel happy for this person, rather than jealous.

Remember that everything exists in the context of reality, just like your life.

5. Learn to be grateful for the life you have.

Remind yourself of the beautiful things in your life—the best memories with friends, at college, or with your family. Make a list of all the positive things that have happened to you (or are STILL happening to you), and notice them as often as you can. This way, you spend more time being grateful, rather than focusing on everything you don't have at the moment.

NOTE THE FOLLOWING: MY PERSONAL FAVORITE AFFIRMATIONS FOR SELF-ESTEEM

And, as aforementioned, to improve your personal self-esteem, you can utilize positive affirmations during the morning or evening. Say them to yourself in the mirror for a more dramatic effect.

I am the most amazing person I can be today.

I am the most loving person I can be today.

I love who I am.

I am enjoying the process of who I am becoming as person.

POSITIVE AFFIRMATION/REMINDERS IN 2ND PERSON FORM

As mentioned previously, changing the tense can have a serious say in how effective your positive affirmations are. If you find greater effects by speaking to yourself with "I," keep it going. However, you can further play around with "you" or just full-out saying your name.

Try the following, placing your name into the sentences whenever you see fit.

Celebrate everything that you are and who you are becoming.

Reach out to others and create happiness and joy in their lives. This will create a like reaction. For every action, there is an opposite reaction.

Close your eyes and focus on your breathing. Think about all the things in your life that you could be grateful for. Imagine waking up each day with a drive to celebrate with the people you love.

Surround yourself with positive and energetic people.

Make everyday a practice of love.

In the next section, learn to speak positive affirmations for greater career success.

Chapter 5. Positive Affirmations for Career Success

Because we live in a fast-paced society, so many of us are looking for ways to improve and become successful in careers and businesses. When it comes to career success, personal growth and development is essential, especially given the stiff competition that exists today. Everyone is working incredibly hard to get to the top. What makes you feel that you're an essential part of the process, of the company? What puts you over the top?

If you find it difficult to answer the previous questions, you need to enhance your interior self-image and internal well-being. This way, you can achieve personal growth and development through improving your mind and your well-being through the use of positive affirmations for career success.

What are Positive Affirmations for Career Success?

As mentioned in previous sections, affirmations are positive thoughts about the desires and outcomes you want to achieve. In order to achieve a heightened level of career success, you should initiate positive affirmations every single day.

Turn to positive affirmations for success when you wake up, when you're driving to your job, or just before you go to sleep—anytime you feel calm and collected, ready to acknowledge your internal self.

Essentially, positive affirmations for career success are aimed to challenge counter-productive or negative thoughts in the workplace. This way, you can fight against those ill-conceived notions that you can't succeed, that you don't deserve a raise, or that you don't deserve a promotion.

WHY SHOULD YOU CREATE POSITIVE AFFIRMATIONS FOR CAREER SUCCESS?

To put it simply: keeping a positive attitude at work can be difficult. People struggle through mundane jobs that they don't like, only to potentially hone their experience to work somewhere they actually like. Thy work places in order to pay their bills, and nothing more. Thusly: that positive attitude can flitter away quite quickly, leaving people shell-like and unable to proceed toward their goals with the appropriate zeal.

While it's true that people can escape their dull work environment through quitting or finding another job, but usually—no matter the position—the next job offers the same constraints. After all: if we don't proceed from job to job with the appropriate mindset, then we won't succeed in our lives at all. We'll live a complain-ridden, humdrum existence.

Affirmations transform your feelings and outlook into something positive. Thusly, the negative feelings you have about your office can transform into something that helps you stay positive and efficient at the workplace.

Furthermore, through these affirmations, you can discard your fears about the workplace—about never reaching your goals—and instead take the appropriate steps, despite the fear.

If you have long or short-term career goals, you must turn to positive affirmations. They set the general moodyou're your workplace mindset, allowing you to walk the walk, so to speak, in achieving your goals.

Thusly, positive affirmations for career success prepare you to fully realize your goals, one step at a time.

How to Create Positive Affirmations for Career Success

Before you begin creating positive affirmations for career success, you must identify the elements that will fuel greater career success.

When you comprehend what you wish to achieve in your career, it's easier to know how you want to proceed. Thusly, if you want a promotion, focus your affirmations around your job. If you want a completely different position, your affirmations should be rooted in another position—one that fulfills what you wish you were doing.

Remember: your affirmations should be straight-forward, clear, and easy to remember.

Examples of Positive Affirmations for Success

Read the following positive affirmations for success every morning, every evening, or every commute to infiltrate this positivity into your "career" mind.

I am successful in everything I do.

I am successful.

I am getting better and better each day.

I will do my best on my job.

I take actions that direct me closer to my goals.

I perform activities relevant to my goals.

I am grateful for the job that I have.

I live with a purpose.

I get myself to take action.

I am successfully attracting the career I want.

A PERSONAL NOTE:

Remember that things will not magically appear in your life. Through these affirmations, you aren't wishfully thinking about what you want. Rather, these affirmations ultimately create "seeds" in your mind that will help you look for every possible way to reach your desired outcome. These seeds help your mind to remain open, ever-searching.

In the next section, learn about positive affirmations for better, stronger relationships.

Chapter 6. Positive Affirmations for Relationships

Positive affirmations lend strength and vitality to so many aspects of your life. Beyond their initial ability to strengthen your career and help you reach toward your goals, they can further help you build and strengthen harmonious relationships. Relationships, in turn, offer so much in terms of confidence and self-worth. Love—both with friends and romantic partners—is like oxygen, the one thing that we all need to feel human, to feel like we belong.

As you work through positive affirmations to enhance the state of your relationship—whatever state that may be—you do not need to make active changes in "real life." Rather, as you make use of these positive affirmations everyday, your subconscious mind will enhance your ability to make this change. Your brain will be more open to the idea of change, and it will fuel you to grow in your relationships.

How to Use Positive Affirmations in Your Relationship

If You're Single and Looking for Stability and Love

When you utilize positive affirmations to find healthy relationships, the affirmations can help attract precisely who you're looking for. They make you open and in the right mindset for these people.

For instance, if you are looking for a life partner, someone who will stay by you and care for you, you could utilize the following affirmation: "I attract individuals who are loving and caring." Through this affirmation, you will naturally begin to attract these individuals. You're willing it.

IF YOU'RE STRUGGLING IN YOUR RELATIONSHIP

If you have a rocky relationship, using positive affirmations can help you fix it and bring it back to stable ground. You need only to tell yourself that you are worthy of the relationship or that you can solve the problem.

Say: "I have a stable and loving relationship."

"My partner and I truly care about each other and bring stability and love to each other's lives."

"All my relationships are friendly, productive, and fun."

"My partner and I are perfectly aligned emotionally and spiritually."

POSITIVE AFFIRMATIONS FOR WORK RELATIONSHIPS

Remember that outside of your home, your work relationships can be some of the most essential—helping you on your path to greater professional success or else pushing you backward, away from your dreams.

As you work through the following positive affirmations, it's essential to remember that at work, people have expectations for you. How well you enact change and growth in your positive at work naturally affects your relationships.

Thusly, you can say something like this—yielding success and building a relationship, all in one:

"I can do my job efficiently in a way that pleases my boss."

"I am an efficient, concise, and resilient worker with great camaraderie with others."

"My work teammates and I have essential teamwork skills that build this company's worth."

SELF-REFLECTION QUESTIONS RELEVANT TO POSITIVE AFFIRMATIONS FOR RELATIONSHIPS

As you think back on your relationships and attempt to build them, structure them, balance them, it's important that you self-reflect on yourself and why these relationships are important to you. Ask yourself:

1. How can I become a better partner and friend?

2. What can I do to have better relationships?

3. Why is my relationship important in my life?

In the next section, you'll learn about positive affirmations that will help you yield a happy and well-rounded life.

Chapter 7. Positive Affirmations for a Happy Life

Remember this: everyone wants happiness. Everyone is seeking it. What's more? The "things" or the people we have in our lives cannot fuel this happiness. (Thusly, if your positive affirmations worked for relationships, for your career, this doesn't automatically mean that you're happy in life. It just means that you've found a bit of success on your path.)

Thusly: happiness is determined through your outlook on life. People in similar situations can have different feelings, depending on their outlook on them.

A great example is found with marriage. After the ceremony, one married person may feel fulfilled as a result of the union, while the other person may feel obliged—forced into the situation by the other. Their outlook on their situation is completely different, which means that their happiness levels are starkly different.

Having a Pleasant Disposition

Although not everybody is born with a pleasant or happy disposition, many experts claim that people can be trained to be happy. Thusly: being happy is a learned "disorder."

In order to be happy, people must simply alter their perception of their world. Through positive affirmations, this altered perception can take form and help change the way people think.

Remember that repeating positive affirmations makes your mind more open to the idea of happiness. It allows you to make affective change, to begin making choices that will, in turn, make you happy. Furthermore, these affirmations can alter your perception on your actions. Thusly: this marriage of good, motivated decisions alongside a happy, full-formed perspective is important on the path to happiness.

ACTIONS TO ENACT HAPPINESS IN YOUR LIFE

As aforementioned, the feeling of "happiness" is brought about through both a shift in perspective and a shift in the actions you do throughout your life.

Certain actions bring happiness to everyday life, including:

1. Expressing gratitude.
2. Doing an act of kindness, such as volunteering at a soup kitchen or even just helping your friend move.
3. Visualizing a good future—on in which you're successful, happy, with that essential perspective on your life that makes you feel that each decision you've made along the way led you to this point.

EXAMPLES OF POSITIVE AFFIRMATIONS FOR A HAPPY LIFE

The following are regular positive affirmations you can use during the morning or during the evening to affirm your positivity and happiness.

I am getting happier and happier each day.

Each day starts with happiness and ends with contentment.

I enjoy every moment of each day.

Repeating Positive Affirmations for a Happy Life

Start your day by affirming yourself with the following:

"I like myself. I love my life. I like myself. I love my life."

It's so essential to tell yourself you like yourself. As mentioned previously—you're the only person you have to hang out with all day. The opinion you have of yourself is the only one that truly matters.

As you say these words, they will manifest into reality. You will grow to appreciate every aspect of your life and yourself—even the rough elements. They're a part of you, and thusly, you should appreciate them.

Ways to Affirm Yourself for a Happy Life

Of course, naturally, things throughout your day can "bring you down" and rally against that happy perspective. In order to fight this sadness, it's essential to fight back against these terrorizing events with the following constructive actions:

1. Respond to every situation in a constructive manner. Thusly, don't wallow in any sense of failure or sadness about them. Enact change.

2. Develop positive thoughts that will neutralize negative feelings or thoughts. Remember: don't allow negative thoughts to rally in your mind for long.

3. Consider setbacks as specific and temporary while staying positive. Remember that they're blockages in the road, ready for you to work through them—tearing them apart stone by stone, so to speak.

4. Welcome various difficulties or trials that come inevitably with achieving happiness. You won't be happy all the time—and that's okay. The "rough" times will offer a perfect juxtaposition to the happy times—making happy times that much more special.

5. Focus on your goals and desires. They're ahead of you, waiting for you to reach them. The future is necessarily more beautiful than today. Keep searching.

Chapter 8. Positive Affirmations for Self-love

You can love your job, love your life; you can love your partner, your friends. And yet: there's one element that's often missing from people—one element that makes all the difference.

Self-love.

Self-love is the single missing ingredient on the path to making positive affirmations truly applicable and successful. Utilize positive affirmations to grow in your self-love, and then naturally make all other positive affirmations stronger.

Hope for a better life for the person you should love and respect: yourself.

Becoming Perfect and Knowing Everything: A Funny Idea, No?

If you are stuck in the idea that you need to be perfect, you are definitely lacking in self-love. After all: nobody in the world is perfect (no matter what your Instagram or Facebook is telling you.)

Positive affirmations can help you reverse the factors that hinder you from loving yourself.

Let's say you're hesitant about starting a relationship. You're unsure if you're capable to maintain and relationship filled with love and understanding, and thus: you won't give yourself a chance.

As a result, positive affirmations work to help you begin believing in your relationship capabilities. You give yourself the strength to love yourself and "see" yourself in that role.

Positive Affirmations for Natural Learning

Know that every single day, you learn something new— about yourself and the outside world. Rather than thinking that you're stupid for not knowing something before, it's essential that you instead comprehend that learning is so natural and essential—as natural as mistakes.

Proceed with the following affirmations:

I forgive myself for making mistakes.

I feel good when others share their talents and knowledge.

I love seeing projects that unfold and go through challenges easily.

Being a Victim

When people are alone, sitting in their room and thinking about their life—usually comparing it to others—they often find themselves calling themselves "victims."

If you find that you do any of the following, you're probably treating yourself as a "victim." This disallows self-love and growth.

1. You spend a lot of energy trying to be treated the way you want.

2. You tell yourself, "I did not have a choice about the matter. I was just forced to do it." You don't own up to your mistakes,

and you blame things on others—even when mistakes are very valid elements of life.

3. You use misfortune as a reason to let others feel guilty. This way, they will help you.

Know that living as the victim doesn't promote a healthy lifestyle in any way. You must own up to your mistakes and affirm yourself in your life role. Through this, you can proceed toward success.

POSITIVE AFFIRMATIONS FOR CREATIVE WISDOM

You will remain at odds with the truth if you think you are powerless or helpless, if you continue to think you're a victim. These affirmations can help you embrace your creative wisdom to empower yourself:

"I am Divinely protected."

"I embody harmony, wisdom, and peace."

"I flow gently on the creative wave of life."

In the next section, learn how positive affirmations can fuel your wealth and prosperity.

Chapter 9. Positive Affirmations for Wealth and Prosperity

Know this: if you think you don't have enough money—if this is you focus—you cannot "create" wealth and prosperity. As mentioned earlier, if you think of only what you lack, you will remain lacking.

However, if you focus your thoughts on the positive—on all the things you do have and your ability to keep growing, you can attract what you desire. If you are grateful for the things you have, you can achieve real wealth and prosperity.

What is Wealth and Prosperity?

Naturally, the meanings of wealth and prosperity differ depending on perception. Perception is everything, as mentioned.

Some people think of prosperity as monetary or material, while others think of wealth as emotional or spiritual. However, the true root of wealth and prosperity stems from having balance in all aspects of life. This includes physical, mental, emotional, and spiritual wealth.

Thusly, wealth and prosperity are experienced only in your mind, rather than externally. There's no Scrooge McDuck leaping into a pool of gold, here.

Your Relationship with Money

If money becomes your goal in life, you tend to forget your real dream. (The one you started out with; the one that initially drove you toward success.)

Think about your beliefs about money. Think about what your parents taught you about money. It is advisable to take time to think about your perception of money. This way, you can recognize any negative perceptions you have about it.

More often than not, negative beliefs come from childhood experiences. For instance, if you were taught: "Money is hard to come by," or "blood and tears is the way to become wealthy," you will continue to grasp for money the hard way.

On the other hand, once you let go of the negative thoughts about money and replace them with positive affirmations, money will come your way. You aren't putting so much "weight" on it, and thus—the stress on yourself is coming off, easing you up to seek better modes of wealth and prosperity.

HOW TO ATTRACT UNLIMITED ABUNDANCE

The world is abundant, and each person deserves a share of that abundance. However, so often, people look out at the world (either consciously or subconsciously) without real belief in that abundance. They certainly don't believe that they should receive any share of it.

If you want to achieve real wealth and prosperity, you need to identify and let go of your underlying beliefs. When you change how you think about the world's wealth, you can eventually change your own reality.

POSITIVE AFFIRMATIONS FOR WEALTH AND PROSPERITY

Read the following positive affirmations to open yourself up to the abundance and prosperity of the world.

I am open with both others and myself.

I accept the abundance of the world unconditionally.

In the next section, work through the 21-Day challenge of positive affirmations to enact real, positive change.

Chapter 10. The 21-Day Challenge: Making Positive Affirmations Work for You

Positive affirmations can condition the subconscious mind to manifest a more positive outlook of your life and yourself. These affirmations can help you accomplish goals, change negative behaviors, or undo damage yielded by negative thoughts and opinions, usually about yourself.

Positive affirmations are easy to make and utilize, especially when coupled with dedication.

21 Days of Positivity and Affirmation

Know that every person's 21-day calendar will look different. It will be personalized to suit their specific needs and required changes.

Thusly, after you've worked through (in previous chapters) what it is you need to change about your life, make a calendar, writing down at least one positive affirmation in each "square" of the calendar. Further, if you please, list your favorite quotes and phrases that will fuel you toward greater positivity.

Each day do one phrase or affirmation through your day as much as possible—morning, commute, lunch break, home commute, and night. Put the list in a place where you will remember—perhaps your cell phone or a small journal.

Create email reminders for yourself and disallow yourself to forget your affirmations of each day.

Read through the following steps to create positive affirmations for your 21-day trial.

STEPS TO MAKE POSITIVE AFFIRMATIONS WORK FOR YOU

STEP 1: IDENTIFY YOUR POSITIVE QUALITIES:

Make an inventory of your best attributes, qualities, and abilities. Starting with "I," write each quality in the present tense. Say, "I am kind," or "I am pretty."

STEP 2: COUNTERACT NEGATIVE THOUGHTS WITH POSITIVE AFFIRMATIONS:

If you have developed a negative perception about yourself, specifically about your abilities or appearance, counteract this perception with positive affirmations. Make a list of the things you want to change.

STEP 3: PRIORITIZE THE THINGS YOU WANT TO WORK ON FROM YOUR LIST:

You might have too many goals. As such, you need to prioritize the most important things first. Concentrate on a few positive affirmations at a time. When you see changes or improvements, move forward to the other things on your list.

STEP 4: WRITE DOWN YOUR POSITIVE AFFIRMATIONS:

The affirmations should be based on positive qualities that you listed on Step 1. Make sure that your affirmations can ultimately influence future improvements or changes.

STEP 5: MATCH SOME OF YOU POSITIVE QUALITIES WITH YOUR DESIRES OR GOALS:

This is the easiest part. You only need to pick out the positive qualities that can help you achieve your set goals.

STEP 6: MAKE YOUR AFFIRMATIONS HANDY:

You need to ensure that your affirmations are always in hand or visible to you. You may never know when you need encouragement. In addition, it is best to repeat your affirmations several times in a day.

STEP 7: REMEMBER YOUR AFFIRMATIONS:

In order to remember your affirmations, it is best to write them down in a diary or journal that you can bring along anytime, anywhere.

Try to meditate on your positive affirmations by closing your eyes, clearing your mind, and simply thinking about the affirmations. Repeat the affirmations as you think about your future.

CONTINUE USING YOUR POSITIVE AFFIRMATIONS

If you continue affirming yourself with positivity, your mind will begin to accept the positivity beyond anything else.

If your goal is short-term, use your positive affirmations until you have achieved it. If you are using affirmations to counteract a negative thought, use them until you feel the negative emotion is pounded to the ground, gone for good.

TIPS TO USE FOR MORE EFFICIENT IMPLEMENTATION OF POSITIVE AFFIRMATIONS

Avoid being discouraged if your affirmations don't seem to help initially. If you get tired of waiting, try to set goals that are reasonable and attainable—rather than the far-reaching, ultimate goals you really want.

If you want to keep your affirmations to yourself, place your reminders in strategic yet discreet locations.

Do not let people pass judgment on your life. Don't let anyone to judge you or weaken your will.

FINAL THOUGHTS: THE BRAIN RETICULAR ACTIVATING SYSTEM

One part of our brain called the reticular activating system (RAS) determines what we notice in our world. When you have a clear vision, enough reasons, repetition, and emotion toward your goal, this RAS takes notice. It essentially states: "I must notice anything that relates to my goal."

This is what you are doing with the 21-day affirmations challenge. You are telling your brain to notice everything related to your desires and goals. This is absolutely essential.

Thusly: affirmations aren't magical. Instead, they're re-conditioning your mind to search the world for elements that will aide you on your path to reach your goals.

POSITIVE QUOTES FROM FAMOUS THINKERS: KEEPING YOU INSPIRED EVERY DAY.

"Finish every day and be done with it. You have done what you could. Some blunders and absurdities no doubt have crept in; forget them as soon as you can. Tomorrow is a new day; begin it well and serenely and with too high a spirit to be cumbered with your old nonsense. This day is all that is good and fair. It is too dear, with its hopes and invitations, to waste a moment on yesterdays." – Ralph Waldo Emerson.

"Every morning you are handed 24 golden hours. They are one of the few things in this world that you get free of charge. If you had all the money in the world, You couldn't buy an extra hour. What will you do with this priceless treasure." – Unknown Quote

"Confucius says Love one another. If it doesn't work, just interchange the last two words."

"People change and forget to tell each other"

– Lillian Hellman

About Justin Albert:

I am all about living life in the moment. I enjoy great company and listening to those who need to be listened to.

I can stay home and have as much fun as when I am out. I find entertainment in the most unique places/things.

I have learned that everything you want in life is right out of your comfort-zone.

This is my personal quote that I live by:

"Waking up each morning excited to start your day and going to sleep each night grateful for every opportunity; regardless of any challenges. Is my definition of success."

ONE LAST FAVOR:

If you enjoyed this book or found it useful I'd be very grateful if you'd post a short review on Amazon. Your support really does make a difference and I read all the reviews personally so I can get your feedback and make this book even better.

If there is anything that you didn't like please feel free to contact me.

At the end of the day, my intend is to help you become the most powerful version of yourself. Please feel free to contact me with questions or if you are in need of advice. My mission is to inspire others.

Thank you for your time!

FREE PREVIEW OF...

BOOST YOUR SELF-CONFIDENCE:

A 21-DAY CHALLENGE TO HELP YOU ACHIEVE YOUR GOALS AND LIVE WELL

JUSTIN ALBERT

WHY YOU SHOULD READ THIS BOOK

This book will help you renew your self-confidence and achieve your potential. It understands the stressors of your past and your present. Memories of your past force you to doubt your sense of self and your abilities in the crowded world around you. You are unable to formulate your own opinions, and you are unable to make new friends. This book's 21-Day Self-Confidence Challenge prescribes a single thing to focus on every day for 21 days. As you focus on your interior life, your exterior life will begin to bubble with positivity. As you renew your mind's strength, you'll see the world with a fresh zeal. You'll want to burst forth, achieve your goals, and reach self-fulfillment. Allow this book to help you take the first steps to rid yourself of past traumas and truly live in the moment.

Chapter 1. Self-Confidence: A Jumping Off Point for the Rest of Your Life

Self-confidence is the most important attribute you can have. It gives you the affirmation to move forward, to reach toward your goals and attain self-actualization. Your potential employers and teachers hope to work with self-confident individuals in order to maintain production in tight schedules. They aspire to work with someone who believes in a wholesome, complete product. All parents hope to create children with complete self-confidence in order to allow them an extra boost in the work and education culture. With self-confidence, you can find yourself living fluidly with friends by your side, with employers speaking to you like an equal rather than an employee. You can operate with new ideas, are unafraid of the future, and accept yourself the way you are.

What is Self Confidence?

Self-confidence is an over-arching attitude. It is a feeling about yourself that allows you to hold ultimate positivity with an assured sense of reality. In other words: it allows you to see the very best of every situation in the proper context. For example, you trust your own abilities and feel in control of your life—to a point. You understand that you cannot do everything; your abilities limit you from certain actions. You may have the ability to play basketball because you have excellent reflexes, have an appropriate height, and can dribble between your legs. These are your abilities. However, these abilities do not transfer to other realms. For example, just because you can dribble between your legs and have incredible height doesn't mean you'll have the ability to swim a mile in a pool. Your abilities transfer only to specific areas of your life, and, if you have self-confidence, you understand the reality of that.

However, your lack of ability in one area does not affect your overall "mission" in the world. You understand your purpose, your goals, and you have the abilities to reach them. You expect to feel respect from your peers for your abilities and goals, and you therefore lend your own respect to your peers for their goals. Furthermore, you maintain a sense of humor. You don't feel the weight of the world; rather, you attain your goals without the undue stress that afflicts the majority of people. Even with your lack of stress, you are hardworking and dependable. You don't have negative stress pushing you to succeed; you simply have a drive to succeed for yourself, for the betterment of your personal goals.

WHEN DO YOU HONE YOUR SELF-CONFIDENCE?

Your self-confidence, or general self-esteem, stems from your very early development: your childhood experiences and the ways you remember them. You'll understand the ways in which these childhood experiences create poor self-confidence in the next chapter. Fortunately, you can drive forward from these past experiences to formulate new ideas of self-confidence, of self-worth. In order to fuel new self-confidence, you must adopt new behaviors. These behaviors must affirm your belief in yourself; they must be action-oriented, ready to charge signals to your brain that you have worth, that you have value. Self-confidence is all about assuring your interior self that your exterior self has value.

CREATING A BOND BETWEEN ACTION AND BELIEF

Your current perception of yourself is your belief-structure. Therefore, if you believe that you're not strong, if you maintain that you're incapable, you lack self-confidence and will therefore find no reason to meet your goals or succeed in your life. Fortunately, your actions can actually alter your beliefs. If you act like someone who is self-confident; if you radiate self-confidence through all you do and say, your actions will begin to feed your perception of yourself. You can alter your interior belief-system and begin to feel like a self-confident person on the inside. This will allow you to reach toward your goals, toward a more zealous sense of self.

Look to the behaviors of a self-confident person and begin to match what they do. Even if your interior self is a little "off" and lacking in self-confidence, you can begin to carry a different posture, a different manner. When your manner aligns with that of a self-confident person, you can feed a better interior sense of self.

6 BEHAVIORS RADIATING IN A SELF-CONFIDENT PERSON

Look for self-confident people in your life and try to understand them a little bit better. They are not naturally self-confident and happy every single day. Everyone has bad days, just like you. However, they understand how to alter their unhappy, not-so-confident days in order to fuel themselves through their actions with sure energy. As you speak with them and monitor their behaviors, try to find all seven of these behaviors in their actions and words.

1. *THEY ARE WILLING TO ACCEPT COMPLIMENTS.*

   When was the last time you didn't sidestep a compliment? Usually, a compliment leaves you spiraling out of control, refuting it. These self-confident people hear expressions of interest, of honor from their peers, and they don't refute them. Instead, they are gracious and accepting. They understand the joys of giving, and they allow their peers to receive that joy of giving by accepting the gift of a compliment. The self-confident people show complete appreciation.

2. *THEY RETAIN POSITIVITY IN EVERY CONVERSATION.*

   How often do you slide from initial greetings to complaints about what you have to do later, how much of a drag your life is right now, or how crappy the weather is? Self-confident people do not slide from positivity. Instead, they discuss their lives with joy and engagement while asking positive-oriented questions of their conversation partner.

3. *THEY VIEW LIMITLESS POTENTIAL AND OPPORTUNITY.*

   How often do you view a life-setback as an opportunity? Probably never. It's difficult to see beyond the initial failure to a new opportunity. Self-confident people, on the other hand, ratchet forward from this initial setback with positivity and a sense of optimism. They view this initial failure as a clean slate, a perfect jumping-off point. They don't allow the failure to rattle their sense of self.

4. *THEY FALL AWAY FROM SELF-PROMOTION.*

   Do you find yourself bragging in order to feel

approval from others? Self-confident people don't feel the need to shout out their accomplishments. They hold complete modesty and do not feel the intense desire to bring attention to themselves. If you find yourself bragging often, you probably feel that you don't deserve respect without calling out for it.

5. *THEY PROJECT INTERNAL CONFIDENCE.*

You recognize a self-confident person when you meet him on the street. He greets you with eye contact and a modest smile. His posture is tall, his gestures are confident. His body language is screaming his self-confidence. How do you talk and walk? Do you walk slowly, slouching? Do you greet people with a smile or a frown? Everything you do either translates your self-confidence or lack of esteem.

6. *THEY ACT AGAINST THEIR DOUBTS WITH POSITIVE ACTION.*

Above, you learned about aligning your beliefs with your actions. Self-confident people do not linger on beliefs that fuel them with doubt. Instead, they take action and boost their production, thus affirming any beliefs that they can do whatever it was they were a bit doubtful about. They busy their minds with solutions rather than their beliefs in the problems.

CHAPTER 2. LACK OF SELF-CONFIDENCE: WHY IT'S NOT YOUR FAULT

Printed in Germany
by Amazon Distribution
GmbH, Leipzig